I believe more in the scissors
than I do in the pencil.

~ *Truman Capote*

Also by James Roethlein

Letters to Roxanne
>	Silver Bow Publishing 2022

An Extravagant Way of Saying Nothing
>	Silver Bow Publishing 2020

Musing on the Cricket Game of Life Part One and a Half
>	Silver Bow Publishing 2018

Writing with Scissors

poems by

James E. Roethlein

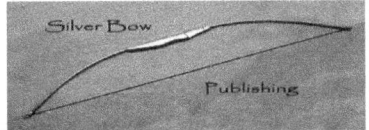

Silver Bow Publishing
720 Sixth Street, Unit # 5
New Westminster, BC
CANADA V3L-3C5

Title: Writing with Scissors
Author: James Roethlein
Publisher: Silver Bow Publishing
Cover Layout and Design: "Blades of Fire" painting by Candice James
Editing: Candice James

All rights reserved including the right to reproduce or translate this book or any portions thereof, in any form without the permission of the publisher. Except for the use of short passages for review purposes, no part of this book may be reproduced, in part or in whole, or transmitted in any form or by any means, either by means electronically or mechanically, including photocopying, recording, or any information or storage retrieval system without prior permission in writing from the publisher or a licence from the Canadian Copyright Collective Agency (Access Copyright).

www.silverbowpublishing.com
info@silverbowpublishing.com
ISBN: 978-1-77403-217-6 paperback
ISBN: 978-1-77403-218-3 electronic book
© 2022 Silver Bow Publishing

Library and Archives Canada Cataloguing in Publication

Title: Writing with scissors / poems by James E. Roethlein.
Names: Roethlein, James, 1971- author.
Identifiers: Canadiana (print) 20220249032 | Canadiana (ebook) 20220249091 | ISBN 9781774032176 (softcover) | ISBN 9781774032183 (EPUB)
Classification: LCC PS3618.O38 W75 2022 | DDC 811/.6—dc23

Author's note:

Most of the poems in this collection are a reflection of my social isolation due to the Covid pandemic. I hope them at least a little bit enjoyable.

Table of Contents

I

A Poem As ... 13
Gilgamesh Remembered ... 14
Craft of the Ages ... 15
A Silenced Hand ... 16
Pen, Paper, Poem ... 17
Poem Dark ... 18

II

Re: Sadness ... 21
My Porcelain Heart ... 22
See Me as I Am ... 23
Beyond Broken ... 24
Get Thee Gone World ... 25
Surrender to the Walls ... 26
An Incomplete View of What Happened ... 27
Stick Figure Boy (Brian's Song) ... 28
Son Shadow ... 29
Silence of Solitude ... 30

III

This Quadriplegic Heart ... 33
This Love in Me ... 34
I, I Am ... 35
Dream Distant ... 36
Even in Dreams ... 37
How Does One...? ... 38
Never to Venture ... 39
Casper Love ... 40
Solitude ... 41

Heart As A Door ... 42
Affection ... 4
Bitter Man, Broken ... 44
The Dating Life of the Insane ... 45
Sahara Heart ... 46
Affection is My Fantasy ... 47
Your Silence Has Been ... 48
Flight to the Moon ... 49
Blood in a Bucket ... 50
Another Poem, Another Drop of Blood ... 51
A Monster with Roses ... 52
Another Moment ... 53
Ashes to Ashes ... 54

IV

Flash Fire Anger ... 57
Dark Symphony 2021 ... 58
Kingdom of Crayons ... 59
Fiddlers On the Roof ... 60
Of Coming Days ... 61
Right Hand, Forehead ... 62
Requiem for Soul Rebellion ... 63
Fisherman on the Churning Sea ... 64
The Width ... 65
Thursday Night ... 66
Hoisted High ... 67
Newborn Spotless Lamb ... 68

V

Live From Vatican Hill ... 71
Penny, Nickel, Dime, Quarter ... 72
A Walk Among the Tombstones ... 73
9/11 ... 74
Of a Day a Lifetime Ago ... 75

Remembrances of Wounded Knee ... 76
Ten Years ... 77
Song for Sydney ... 78
Morning Majestic ... 79

VI

Death Valley Rainstorm ... 83
60% Chance of Snow, Then Nothing ... 84
My Foot Is Asleep ... 85
My Relationship with You ... 86
Paces the Air ...87
Windswept Days ... 88
I Woke Up This Morning ... 89

VII

Thirty Years ... 93
He Sacrificed His Eyes ... 94
Honey and Heaven ... 95
He Would Dream of Her ... 96

I

A Poem As...

A poem as razor blades
sackcloth tuxedos
and essence of ashes,
bloodletting verse,
like leeches
and medieval medicine,
soothing as sandpaper
erasing blackboard chalk.
With bleeding ears
(sound assaulted),
you, in Idol fashion
cry for more
cry for more
cry for more.

Gilgamesh Remembered

Gilgamesh remembered,
a little man carving notches in stone,
lost to mists of time.

Odysseus remembered,
Homer honored and Virgil for Aeneas,
both escaping time's oblivion.

Poets remembered
in this era devoid of mythical heroes,
and the stories forgotten.

Craft of the Ages

Bound in time,
eternities created,
cuneiform set in stone,
ink upon the printed page,
reread, revisited,
eternities to shape the future
and define the past,
poems, prose, plays, and songs.
But before them,
paintings on cold cave walls.

A Silenced Hand

A silenced hand
a voice rendered still,
and words will suddenly stop
the way rivers remain running.

For writers write
living on borrowed time,
never knowing which word is last
before drawing their final breath.

But they live on
through the printed page,
until no one reads anymore
and the world slips into oblivion.

Pen, Paper, Poem

Pen, paper, poem.
Pen, paper, poem,
how they flow,
word sharpened swords
both battle-axe and balm
for the world,
for the world,
edification, amusement
to ears and eyes
   ears and eyes,
as the poet writes on,
bleeding rivers of lemon juice
heat revealed
no one cares to see
and the poet fades,
roses in winter,
frostbitten and withered,
forgotten ...
forgotten.

Poem Dark

Poem dark,
night surrounded, written
in a light starved room,
words reflecting a winter fog,
frozen, thick and rolling
thru streets of soul and mind.

The poet's heart as iceberg,
deep and dangerous,
cursed, so cursed, but loved
for what they are, not who they are.

And knowing this,
John died
Anne died
Sylvia died.

II

Re: Sadness

The trespass

The pain

The tears

Love broken, bleeding

taken away

never given

never allowed to be given

We hold a mirror to the world
forcing it to see what it is

My Porcelain Heart

My porcelain heart; shattered,
in the way of the watching world,
and settling on one of plasticware,
I live a dying life
        without music,
                without poetry,
                      without love.

See Me As I Am

See me as I am
and run away,
supernovas and black holes,
all that fills these eyes.

See me as I am
and run away,
my heart as a grease fire
and twice as pleasing.

See me as I am
and run away,
a roadside banana, rotten,
blackened by a summer sun.

See me as I am
and run away,
    run away,
    run away.

Beyond Broken

Beyond his broken love-starved heart,
he fears the eyes of the mirror man
and the shadow soul hidden beneath
(speaking in velvet barbed-wire whispers).
He listens,
He listens
        and dies to the world,
          then dies to himself ...

              ALONE

Get Thee Gone World

Momentary pause,
an East Shore life, turned
to a West Bank existence,
home is more than refuge,
where I go, where I go,
to hide away from the world.

Thirty turns, five and two,
progeny eyes, longing, failing
to see that paternal face
now grave gone and dead.

Roxanne speaking to Cyrano,
such a great catch, but,
impassioned love, second fiddle
to lava, and volcanic ash,
and the other man who hurt you.

I walk away (stone and a hill),
cold and cut off to shadows,
Medusa eyes left behind to stare
at this get thee gone world,
and I'm the bitter one.

Surrender to the Walls

Surrender to the walls
surrender to the silence,
gargoyles guarding
the empty spaces between.
The world in mime whispers,
says "get thee gone", and he does,
fading along solitude's road
from human touch, human sympathy.

An Incomplete View of What Happened

Borrowed breath,
you breathed mine
and I faint fell
from the serpentine
of your feigned affections.
This quartz heart of mine
(rendered metamorphic)
turned to sandstone,
and Atlas failed
to hold up the sky.

Five years fooled, finally
forced to say; no more.

Stick Figure Boy (Brian's Song)

He was
the stick figure boy
He was
the stick figure boy
He was
the stick figure boy,
gangly,
and a little weird.

The things
we had done to him
The things
we had done to him
The things
we had done to him,
being,
cruel without the kind.

We then
drove Brian away
We then
drove Brian away
We then
drove Brian away,
and I,
was knee deep in it.

Son Shadow

The courier came too late,
delivering news by spider's web
and wrong turns at Albuquerque.
A tombstone waits, years in vain
for son shadow to darken it.

Silence of Solitude

Silence of solitude
(still as sails with no wind),
seasons spent separated,
the endless repetitions of
living below the poverty line
of love and relationship.
Dying, I carry my coffin
for a funeral, with no one
(but birds and empty air)
to mourn my passing.

III

This Quadriplegic Heart

This quadriplegic heart
gone the way of the dinosaur,
deprived, feeling deceasing,
mind and body carrying on
as one dead and existing.

Solitary isolation my prison shroud,
worn, and no one comes near,
tender touches and tender words,
memories confined to a fading past
as I embrace loneliness like a lover.

This Love in Me

This love in me,
slipping from
ten beats a lifetime
down to none,
soul in cardiac arrest,
shattered shell of self,
slow decline, slow descent,
the dead, amongst the living.

I, I am...

I,
I am,
I am the stuff of nightmare dreams,
haunting your steps ev'ry inch and hour
with the constant unwanted cries
of love me,
   love me,
    love me.

Dream Distant

Dream distant, far from here
as the outer edge of forever.
This lady he would love
is ever west of where he walks,
and he, is always travelling east.

Even in Dreams

Even in dreams
she walks away,
leaving this heart
in an earthen pot,
Pompeii buried,
faded and forgotten.

How Does One...?

How does one walk away
    when you,
           when you ...

were
    never
        there?

Never to Venture

Never to venture
that far north to her,
a 38th parallel,
Roddenberry neutral zone.
And he shall be, he shall be
(always to her),
never a lover, just a friend.

Casper Love

Casper love,
friendly, but still a ghost,
equally unseen,
unheard as the blind
listening to street mimes,
never enough,
never enough,
for one longing
to hold you, to be held,
kisses at night and caresses,
something sensual,
longer than one night stands
and bleeding into years,
of ordinary days.

Solitude

Another tear un-cried,
its wellspring buried deep,
cast to an emotional oblivion
and he ceases to weep.

A slow death, heart frozen,
rendered unwilling, incapable
of what the world feels
and takes for granted.

Solitude is his reward,
the end of his everything.

Heart As A Door

Heart as a door,
rain-rusted, warped,
frozen to a touch,
unending nights
in silenced solitude
beneath a wintry sky
of lunar light eclipses.

Heart as a door,
too far gone to ever care
should love come knocking.

Affection

Nail me
to the wall,
affection,
my war crime,
and you ...
and you
are my judge
at Nuremberg.

Bitter Man, Broken

Bitter man, broken,
dreams the stuff
of obsidian shadow,
red roses black,
wilted petals
and cry-me-rivers
of blood painted thorn.

Desert man, enduring
a hollowed out heart
clothed in cactus love
and sandstorm affection
wanders away
from human kindness
then just
wanders away,
wanders away.
wanders away ...

TO DIE

The Dating Life of the Insane

If I like her
I will ask her,
and she, will tell me no.
Rinse
Dry
Repeat

Sahara Heart

What can he know of love,
wandering from pool to pool
in the Sahara of his heart?

If he wanted her full and deep,
she'd whisper back night and day
how much she felt the same.

How little he knows the ways
of affection in a fallen world, thinking
what he gives will be given back.

And so he wanders, disillusioned,
turning weather worn and stone,
repelling any glimpses of tenderness.

Affection Is My Fantasy

Affection is my fantasy,
dreams ne'er meant to be.
Reality is a wasteland,
arsenic on roses
and thorns that are bleeding.
Mention me, I'm porcupine quills
only able to puncture, to wound
hope hidden in your name
and mar the heavens I've seen
in your emerald Gemini eyes.

Your Silence Has Been

Your silence has been
a cancer on my heart,
removing you has been
an emotional mastectomy.

Flight to the Moon

She thought,
he'd take her to the moon
(that first night together),
how little she marveled
(when she saw),
how, like a failed rocket
he was more than unable
to leave the launching pad,
let alone ascend into orbit.

Blood in a Bucket

Another drop, blood in a bucket,
bloodshot inward shadow eyes
(in Augustine fashion)
are staring long at the flaws
of a past he never forgets
and holds as a sword to fall upon daily.

World weary, weakened,
a broken man wandering a broken road,
closes his eyes to hear love
flowing from the lips of a mime,
then mixes his laughter with his tears,
when a normal man would simply cry.

Another Poem, Another Drop of Blood

Another poem
another drop of blood,
red rum eyes in the mirror
and Cyrano writes to woo you
while wearing a phantom mask
to cover his darker side.
A naked nose, a disfigured face,
and like the raven gently rapping
upon your door,
upon your door,
upon your door ...
will you dare to let him in?

A Monster with Roses

A monster with roses in his hands,
is still a monster,
and he will force-feed you thorns,
sugar-coated and chocolate dipped,
turning your window eyes
bloodstained and cracked.

Then leaves you when he chooses,
your soul sickened, body broken
and bleeding upon the floor.

Another Moment

Another moment
pottery cracked,
and where,
is the gold to mend it?

Emotion walls
weathered
and desert worn,
brittle, breaking,
accused of what
he did not do,
    did not do ...,
or can't remember.

Ashes To Ashes

Ashes to ashes,
sunlight for a vampire heart
destined to become dust,
the fragile undead thing
loathing a peaceful life
of men and women together.

Hashtag mass approval
to bring them all down,
make them burn,
make them burn,
'til all the world withers
when men give up,
give up and walk away,
from you; and your revenge.

IV

Flash Fire Anger

Flash fire anger
and verbal swords,
this is how men die
and brutal war begins.

Dark Symphony 2021

Further down our rabbit hole
descending to free fall,
the abyss beckons
and there is no wonderland
(only the nine circles).

In these days of now,
dark waters
(midst the mob demanding justice done)
defend blade and bullet bearers
(blood letting upon their own)
from the stream stemming the tide
of red rivers staining the streets.

We continue,
we continue ...
ignoring the yesteryears,
and advance to soul oblivion
beyond our world's final breath.

Kingdom of Crayons

In the Kingdom of crayons
it's midnight blue against black,
and we follow suit,
going to war
with different hues of wax.

An orange face,
an orange face,
there, to place our blames upon.

All the while, the Devil's
on the inside looking in,
and he is laughing,
        laughing,
          laughing.

Fiddlers On the Roof

We are as fiddlers on the roof,
shackled to the shifting sand standards
of a generation rooted in the wind
(this is right, then this is wrong).

We live a moral life as bumper cars,
going this way and that,
suffering more than we prosper ...
the slow death of a frog boiled in water.

Of Coming Days

The sevenfold sea burning,
continental chaos
born of gun powder, gasoline,
and a quarter caught away.

Appeasement in turn comes,
a solitary ship
(ten banners beneath its own)
for a single week of years.

Right Hand, Forehead

Right hand, forehead.
Right hand, forehead,
cattle-branded, much like
the way we've been vaxxed,
and our future walking sticks,
nearly whittled,
nearly ready for Armageddon.

Requiem for Soul Rebellion

Hellfire,
waiting beyond
eternity's veil,
screams
and oblivion air,
the burning ...
the burning
of soul inferno,
and no escaping
the nine circles
descending,
down, down,
to freezing fire
of two faces
tormenting pain.

Elohim eyes
looking away,
looking away...
'til forever ends.

Fishermen on the Churning Sea

Fishermen on the churning sea,
boats upon the verge
of seven minutes 'til midnight.
What will they do?
What will they do ...
waiting for the trumpet sound,
the ocean calling them home?

The Width

The width
of a thousand oceans
spans the gulf,
separating us from Eden.

Blood flowed,
love covering the curse
on the sons of Adam
and daughters of Eve.

Thursday Night

Body – blood
wafers – wine,
praises turned crucifixion.

A mother's milk gone sour
to boil its lamb son alive.

We lament, and remember
(upon this Thursday night)
the actual retail price paid,
the victory won from defeat.

Hoisted High

Hoisted high,
world watching
with crucifixion eyes,
parched lips
and vinegar wine.

Belabored breaths,
suff'ring 'til the final gasp,
as seven things
spoken, crescendos
to whispered screams.

Newborn Spotless Lamb

Newborn spotless lamb
swaddling wrapped
(as custom demands)
sleeps on stone,
precious, protected,
born predestined for sacrifice,
three set upon a stone, then
RISEN
RISEN
RISEN.

V

Live From Vatican Hill

Hanging upside down
from a Roman tree,
nailed and dying
Peter is seeing the world
in its natural perverted way.

Penny, Nickel, Dime, Quarter

Penny, nickel, dime, quarter,
measures of remembrance
for the fallen, crowns of honor
adorning headstones,
such a small sacrifice of memorial
for those paying the ultimate price.

A Walk Among the Tombstones

A walk among the tombstones,
marble teeth memorials
of the dead uttering to the eyes
"remember us".

But with the day's worries
being enough for the day,
we lend them a passing ear,
giving them a passing thought.

9/11

Death on such a grand scale,
three buildings,
a hole in a field.

All these years after
and still crying.

How can we forget?
How can we forget?

Of a Day a Lifetime Ago

A man,
a rifle,
a Dallas motorcade.

And then,
a nation mourning.

Remembrances of Wounded Knee

It was a beautiful dream
that ended in the silence
of the dead laying
huddled and scattered
upon the winter ground.

Ten Years

Ten years,
ten years gone by,
and still,
I miss mommy.
I miss mommy.

Song for Sydney

Call him Mister.
Call him defiant one,
the man departed
in the heat of the night
for the lilies of the field
on the other side.

And in his leaving
like a raisin in the sun,
the world is left
both richer and poorer.

Morning Majestic
"for God; is a creative artist"- Toby Mac

Morning majestic,
sunrise over savanna and sea,
lofty mountains, lightning storms
peering down on the valleys
and rainforests below.

Look and see where God is found,
He is here too,
among the pigments of His palette,
this throng of humanity
living in their manufactured world.

VI

Death Valley Rainstorm

I got dry,
as I got wet.

60% Chance of Snow, Then Nothing

The entire poem tucked in a title,
but I'm taking you for a little ride
and talking about something else.

My Foot Is Asleep

My foot is asleep
but my cats are not,
and they are walking,
walking all over me.

My Relationship With You

I give
and you take.
I give
and you take.
I give
and you take.

This relationship,
built on what I do for you,
and you give little back,
a look, a word (in your fashion)
should I step out of line.

And still,
and still,
I (like the ancient Egyptians)
obey you ...
my feline masters.

Paces the Air

Paces the air,
winged race-car driver,
twelve inches
to rent the space overhead.

I duck and cover
to end this poem,
but not the story.

Wind Swept Days

Wind swept days,
a world, window opposite,
so cold, so bitter,
winter cloud reflections,
and Jack is waiting,
waiting with frost fingers
to claim and carry me
to his season,
his realm of ice.

I Woke Up This Morning

I woke up this morning,
and I woke up.
I woke up this morning,
and I woke up.
I woke up this morning,
but I was dreaming,
dreaming ...
about waking up this morning.

VII

Thirty Years

Thirty years he poured a cup,
tea and a table setting
for an empty chair
like a crutch without an owner,
a silenced voice (mortal coil claimed)
faded, unforgotten sight and sound.

Thirty years he never loved another
(Death unable to truly part them),
'til the time Christmas Present came
no longer able to find him.

He Sacrificed His Eyes

He sacrificed his eyes
to be her ever forever,
for he saw her beauty
hidden deep beneath
the snakes for hair
and turn to stone gaze
that was her curse.

Honey and Heaven

Queen
of my days.
Goddess
of my nights,
come unto me
in this little
corner of country,
if only
to speak to me
in a tongue
lashing mood
I deserve,
that I may see,
that I may hear
the honey and heaven
of your eyes,
of your face,
of your voice.

He Would Dream of Her

He would dream of her
and woo her in metaphor,
likening her loveliness
to a newly fallen snow
and meadow flowers
in the summertime.

He would dream of her
and woo her in metaphor,
for she is the dew
on the early morning grass,
and the wind in the trees
whistling the air around him.

He would dream of her
and woo her in metaphor,
speak of her mirror eyes,
and lose himself
staring into the heavens
he sees reflected there.

www.ingramcontent.com/pod-product-compliance
Lightning Source LLC
Chambersburg PA
CBHW070307120526
44590CB00017B/2582